Pine Creek

D0115283

Pine Creek Church Library

Simple

SIMPLE SERMONS ON PRAYER
Ford W. Hershel
Pine Creek Church Library

Date   Name

Pine Creek Church Library

Simple Sermons on Prayer

Herschel W. Ford

BAKER BOOK HOUSE

Grand Rapids, Michigan 49506

Copyright 1969 by
The Zondervan Corporation,
Grand Rapids, Michigan.

Reprinted 1985 by
Baker Book House Company,
Grand Rapids, Michigan,
with permission of the
copyright holder.

ISBN: 0-8010-3520-1

Printed in the United
States of America

This book is dedicated
in love and gratitude
to all those precious friends
who have prayed for me
over the years of my
ministry for Christ.
"I thank my God upon
every remembrance" of them.

Foreword

I do not claim any special originality in these messages. I collected the material for them over many years and have used them in my preaching ministry. I hope that, through the reading of these simple sermons, someone may be led into a deeper prayer life and a closer walk with God.

Preachers and other Christian workers are certainly free to use anything in this book as their very own, and may God bless them as they do.

W. HERSCHEL FORD

Contents

Simple
Sermons
on
Prayer

1

The Christian's Prayer Life

Matthew 6:5-7; James 4:2, 3

The Christian is a person of many high privileges. There are some people who think that the life of a Christian is completely devoid of any privilege. They believe that when one becomes a Christian he gives up every joy, and his life becomes barren, humdrum and sad. Just the opposite is true. The Christian has many sweet privileges which the unbeliever never has. He has the privilege of going to the Bible and reading God's love-letter to his heart. He has the privilege of going to church and hearing a gospel message that will help him to live a better and sweeter life. He has the privilege of fellowship with the finest people on earth — God's people. He has the privilege of giving his substance that others might come to know Christ. He has the privilege of serving in the only army that will be ultimately victorious.

But the Christian's sweetest privilege is the privilege of talking to God, for that's what prayer is. It's a sad day in the Christian's life when he begins to neglect his prayer life. It is as if God had given us a blank check which He had signed, and we tear up the check. It is as if God had given us the key to His great heavenly storehouse, and we threw the key away. Are you neglecting this privilege?

There are powers in a Christian's life. There is power in what a man is. If he is living close to Jesus he has a power that others do not have. It was a dark and gloomy day in Boston. The next day a reporter wrote these words in the paper, "It was a dark and gloomy day yesterday. Then Phillips Brooks walked through our office and the sun began to shine." Oh, the power of a Christian life! Has anyone's day been made brighter by your life? Is anyone's life influenced by your life? Does anyone want to live for Christ because he has seen Him living in you?

There is power in what a man says. Just think of the power that great preachers have wielded with words through the centuries. But you don't have to be a public figure to have power in your words. Everyone has this power. It can be a power for good or bad. In one of my churches we were about to elect a certain man as a deacon and ordain him to this high office. But we learned that he used profane language on his job, so we did not elect him. We knew that his profanity would bring reproach to the cause of Christ, and God can't use you if your speech is not what it ought to be.

There is power in what a man does. Jesus "went about doing good," and that gave Him a mighty power among the people. While He went about doing good, some of us just "go about." But today, as a man does good in the name of Jesus, he is given greater power and greater influence.

Billy Graham wanted to be a big-league baseball player, but God got hold of him and today he is the world's foremost evangelist. Now he might have become the greatest player in the history of baseball, but he would not have the power and influence he has today. What a man does gives him power.

There is power in what a man gives. If I withhold my money and my time and my talent from the world, I will have no power. I will die and no man will miss me. But if I use these things for the Lord I can make a contribution that will bless the world.

Surely man's greatest power is the power of prayer. The man who prays is a thousand times stronger than the man who doesn't pray. "Satan trembles when he sees the weakest saint upon his knees." Kingdoms have been won, souls have been saved, churches have been built, lives have been blessed and changed because of prayer. The sick have been healed and prodigals have been brought home because of prayer. Homes have been changed and marriages saved because of prayer. Many marvelous things have been wrought by prayer.

I. What Does the Bible Promise Concerning Prayer?

1. *Forgiveness for sins.* "If we confess our sins, he is faithful and just to forgive us our sins, and to cleanse us from all unrighteousness" (I John 1:9). We sin daily; something is always coming up between us and God. How can we get it out? By coming to God in prayer, by confessing our sins and asking for God's forgiveness.

David was a man after God's own heart, but he sinned greatly. Later his heart was broken, and he lost all the joy of salvation. How did he find peace? He found it when he prayed for forgiveness. Listen to that prayer in Psalm 51:1 - 3, "Have mercy upon me, O God, according to thy lovingkindness: according unto the multitude of thy tender mercies blot out my transgressions. Wash me throughly from mine iniquity, and cleanse me from my sin. For I acknowledge my transgressions: and my sin is ever before me." What a prayer! Did God answer that prayer? Yes, He answered the prayer and restored to David the joy of His salvation, so that David could sing, "Blessed is he whose transgression is forgiven, whose sin is covered" (Psalm 32:1).

2. *A supply of wisdom.* We need wisdom greatly today for we are living in a complex and confused age. Every day there are many decisions to be made. And God promises to direct us if we call on Him. "If any of you lack wisdom, let him ask of God, that giveth to all men liberally, and upbraideth not; and it shall be given him" (James 1:5).

3. *Divine healing.* I believe in divine healing, but I don't believe in professional "divine healers." I have stood by the bedside of those whom the doctors had given up. I have prayed and others have prayed and the Lord brought these people out well and strong. It is amazing how God answers prayer for the sick, according to His will. "And the prayer of faith shall save the sick, and the Lord shall raise him up; and if he have committed sins, they shall be forgiven him" (James 5:15).

4. *The provision for our needs.* "Be careful for nothing; but in every thing by prayer and supplication with thanksgiving let your requests be made known unto God" (Philippians 4:6).

5. *The answer to covenant prayer.* "Again I say unto you, That if two of you shall agree on earth as touching any thing that they shall ask, it shall be done for them of my Father which is in heaven" (Matthew 18:19).

Dr. George W. Truett preached on this text at a morning service in a revival. At the close of the service a woman stood up and said to him, "Preacher, do you believe what you have preached this morning?" He answered, "Yes, I have preached the Word of God." "Well," said the woman, "I wonder if you would covenant with me to the end that my husband should be saved in this revival. He is a steamship captain on the river. He is lost. I long to see him saved in this very revival. Will you covenant with me on the promise in this text?" The preacher hesitated, for this was a big order. Then a man on the other side of the church from the woman stood up and said, "Lady, I believe that promise. I will covenant and pray with you for your husband's salvation." He walked toward the front of the church and she met him there. As they stood before the pulpit they prayed their first covenant prayer, basing it on this promise.

That night the woman came to church, bringing her unsaved husband with her. The preacher said that he poured out his heart that night for the soul of that one man, but the man did not respond to the gospel invitation. But as the people left the church the woman and the man smiled at each other, as if to say, "We know God will keep His promise." The next morning, as the great preacher prayed in the pastor's study, there came a knock upon the door. He opened the door and there was the steamship captain. He said, "Preacher, I cannot wait until the morning service, tell me how to be saved." The man was soon rejoicing in Christ and came forward in church that morning to joyfully confess Christ as his Saviour and Lord.

Do you bear a heavy burden on your heart? Then covenant with someone else and pray. Storm the gates of heaven. God answers every true prayer in one of three ways. He may answer "Yes," and that is wonderful. That is the time to fall on your knees and thank Him. He may answer, "No," and that's a wise answer. If your baby cried out for a red-hot coal of fire you would say "No." That would be the best answer. And when God says "no," it is because He knows what is best for you. Or He may say, "Wait a while, you are not yet ready for this." But He does answer every true prayer.

Yes, the Bible is full of promises concerning prayer. God's ear is always open to our pleas; His heart is always receptive to our cry.

II. Why Do We Pray?

1. *To get things from God.* Someone will say, "But that is selfish; that is the wrong motive. We are to pray in order to maintain a spiritual relationship to God." While that is surely true, we also pray in order to get things from God. The Bible tells us over and over to ask God for the things we need. When our younger son went back to college to work toward his doctor's degree, he had a wife and a baby daughter. I told him that I didn't want him to do without the things that he and his family needed. I told him to C.O.D. — call on dad. And believe me, he did. If I will do that for my son, how much more will our heavenly Father do for His children. He knows that we are needy creatures, and He tells us to call on Him for what we need.

Study the prayers of the Bible and you'll see how much "asking" there is in them. Jesus gave us the "model prayer." It is contained in five verses in the Bible, but there are six requests, six "askings" in these five verses, all the way from asking for daily bread to the coming of His kingdom on earth.

I had a wife and two children when I went to Wake Forest College. I was called, at a small salary, to a little church forty miles from the campus. I was forced to borrow $300 from a big bank in Raleigh, North Carolina, on the endorsement of one of my deacons. I kept a small bank account for groceries and other expenses in the bank at Wake Forest. One day the news came that the big bank had failed and I was still indebted to them for the $300. I went down to the small bank where I kept our expense money and asked them if the failure of the big bank would affect them. They assured me that my account was perfectly safe, that the bank was solvent.

But when I went to the post office the next morning I saw a crowd in front of the little bank and learned that it had also failed. I had $1.05 in my pocket and no more money for our expenses. Now in Atlanta there was a good woman who always sent me a book on my birthday or at Christmas time. When I reached the post office I found a letter from her. She said, "I didn't know what book to buy you this Christmas, so I am sending you $5.00 and you can buy the book you want." Let me tell you that $5.00 did not go for books, but for living expenses. It was that way all through those lean years. Then came graduation time. We were in the church on Sunday morning for the commencement sermon. As we stood to sing the doxology, "Praise God from whom all blessings flow," the tears flowed down my cheeks, and I found myself thanking God for bringing us through. Afterward my wife told me that she felt the same way.

> What a friend we have in Jesus,
> All our sins and griefs to bear!

What a privilege to carry
Everything to God in prayer!
O what peace we often forfeit,
O what needless pain we bear,
All because we do not carry
Everything to God in prayer!

2. *To prevent worry.* Some people worry about everything. It is evident that they don't pray enough. I have already quoted Philippians 4:6, where we are told not to worry about anything, but to come to God in prayer. Worry is sinful for a Christian. God has promised to take care of His children. If we worry about what is going to happen to us — if we doubt God — we show a lack of faith, and that is sinful.

John Wesley said, "I would no more worry than I would curse or swear." Hear the cry of the man in Psalm 34:6, "This poor man cried, and the Lord heard him, and saved him out of all his troubles." Isn't that better than worrying? Take your burdens to the Lord and leave them there.

3. *To keep in close touch with God.* You have a friend in the city. You see him every day; you eat with him once a week; you have sweet fellowship with him. Then he is transferred; he moves a thousand miles away. You both promise to write often to each other. You keep this up for awhile, then the letters grow farther and farther apart. Soon you correspond only at Christmas time. You find other friends and other interests and soon you have almost forgotten your old friend. It's the same way in the spiritual realm. You walk and talk with God and He seems very near. Then someone moves. It isn't God, it's you. Soon you cease to pray and God seems far away. There is only one cure for such a situation. We must stay close to God in prayer.

III. Why Are Our Prayers Not Answered?

1. *They are not offered.* "Ye have not, because ye ask not" (James 4:2). Henry Ford had a friend in the insurance business, but one day Mr. Ford bought a million dollar policy from another insurance agent. His friend called him and asked why he didn't buy the policy from him. Mr. Ford replied, "You didn't ask me." In Psalm 107 we are told how men go down to the sea in ships. Then when the storm arises and the waves mount up toward heaven, the sailors begin to cry out for God. It's the same with the average Christian. When life is running smoothly he forgets God, when trouble arises he cries out to his Maker.

I read of a group of miners who had been entombed for several days in the depth of a mine. When they were rescued someone asked them what they did during those days in the bosom of the earth. And they said, "We prayed all the time." And I wondered how much they prayed when they were not in any danger.

2. *We pray with the wrong motive.* "Ye ask, and receive not, because ye ask amiss, that ye may consume it upon your lusts" (James 4:3). God looks at the motive behind our prayers. When we pray we need to ask ourselves, "Why am I praying for this? What will I do with the answer when it comes?" You ask God for good health, but will you use that strong body in His service? You ask for a better job, but will you witness rightly for the Lord in that new job? You ask for more money, but will you give God His part of that money? We must not pray simply for something so that we can consume the answer on ourselves. We must remember God in it all.

3. *We pray with the wrong spirit in our hearts.* David said, "If I regard iniquity in my heart, the Lord

will not hear me" (Psalm 66:18). Mrs. H. V. Bamberger was the wonderful and devoted church visitor of the First Baptist Church of El Paso, when I served there as pastor. During the days of the deep depression her husband worked for $18.00 per week. One night his boss came to see him and the talk drifted around to taxes. Mr. Bamberger stated that he had paid his tax. The boss said, "How could you pay your tax? I haven't been able to pay mine." Mr. Bamberger said, "We live very simply, we take out a dollar here and a dollar there, and we pay our taxes that way." The boss went home and called Mr. Bamberger and said, "You're better off than I am; you need not come to work tomorrow." And there were the Bambergers in the midst of the depression, with no job. Mrs. Bamberger became bitter toward the man who had fired her husband. She prayed for her husband to find a job, but her prayers were not answered. Then one Sunday her pastor preached on the sin of Achan. He said that God would not answer our prayers and bless us if we had sin in our hearts. His statement made this dear woman see the sin that was in her heart, the sin of a wrong attitude toward that man. She was cut to the quick. She went home, got down on her knees and asked God to forgive her. On Monday morning she went down to the man's office, confessed her wrong to him and asked him to forgive her. Then she could really pray with "nothing between." The next day her husband got the best job he had ever had.

4. *We are not abiding in Christ and keeping His commandments.* "If ye abide in me, and my words abide in you, ye shall ask what ye will, and it shall be done unto you" (John 15:7). Dr. J. A. Campbell was a great old preacher in North Carolina. Campbell College is named for him. When his two sons were of col-

lege age he took them to Wake Forest College to enroll them. Before he left them he said to them, "I am going to leave my checkbook with you. As long as you live as I have taught you to live, you can make out these checks for your expenses and I will cover the checks when they come back to the bank in our little town. I am not wealthy, but I will do my best for you as long as you live up to the Christian principles I have taught you." And for the college years the boys lived godly lives, and their father honored the checks and furnished them the things that they needed.

This is a perfect illustration of this verse. As long as you and I are living rightly for God, abiding in Christ and keeping His commandments, we can call upon Him and He will supply our needs. But He does not promise His supply to those who break His commandments and live apart from Him.

5. *We are not earnest enough.* Moses cried out to God, "Answer my plea for Israel or blot me out of Thy book." Jacob said, "I will not let Thee go unless You bless me." John Knox said, "Give me Scotland or I die." The Bible says, "The effectual fervent prayer of a righteous man availeth much" (James 5:16).

6. *We do not believe they are going to be answered.* When I was in college my younger son told me one night that he had prayed for God to send him a white, shaggy dog. I wondered why Robert would pray such a prayer for he knew I could not buy him a dog. But the next Sunday one of the members of the little church where I preached said to me, "Our Spitz dog had some puppies about eight weeks ago, and we want to give one to your boys." And Robert had his white, shaggy dog. He had faith that God would answer his prayers.

7. *We are not submissive to God's will.* Dr. L. R. Scarborough was preaching in a revival in a certain

church. An attractive young lady came up to him and said, "I want you to pray for my unsaved father. I want to see him saved in this revival." Dr. Scarborough said to her, "Is God calling you to any special service?" The young lady bowed her head and said, "Yes, He has called me to be a missionary, but I am not going to leave my family and my home and my friends and go to some foreign country." Then Dr. Scarborough said, "Young lady, as long as you have that attitude I am afraid your father won't be saved." He said that he saw scores of people saved in that revival, but the young woman's father was unmoved.

God may not call you to be a preacher or a missionary or to occupy some prominent public position. But He may be calling you to some work in the church, to teach a class, to sing in the choir, to lead some young people. He may be calling you to establish a family altar, to tithe, to go out and witness to a neighbor. As long as you remain disobedient to Him your prayers will go unanswered.

As far as possible we ought to have a definite time and a definite place for our daily prayers. Then we should live the rest of the day in the atmosphere of prayer, so that at any time we can reach out and touch the hem of His garment.

Then we ought to pray in the right spirit, saying always, "Here I am, Lord. Whatever You choose for me, let me choose for myself." And of course every prayer should be offered in the name of Jesus Christ and for His glory.

In the Civil War a well-to-do couple lost their only son. Their sorrow was overwhelming. They shut themselves up with their grief and refused to see anyone. One day a young man rang their doorbell and asked to see them. The butler told him that they would see no one, that they had suffered a great loss. The young man pulled a letter out of his pocket and said, "Take this in to them." The butler carried the letter in to the couple. The man trembled as he saw the handwriting on the letter. "Look mother," he said, "this is our son's handwriting."

He read the letter with trembling hands and quivering lips. "Dear father and mother:" the letter said, "The man who brings you this letter was my best friend in the army. He helped me on many occasions. Now in what I believe will be my last hours he is with me. If he ever comes your way, give him the best you have, for your son's sake." You know what that couple did, don't you? They took that young man in and gave him the best they had, for their son's sake.

Our Father in heaven is rich, He holds the wealth of the world in His hands. He has all we need and is ready and willing to supply those needs. So come now and call upon Him and He'll give you the best He has, for His Son's sake.

2

Prayer Changes Things — and People

Acts 4:31

Before prayer we can do little — after prayer we can do much. Much effort without prayer often results in failure — the same effort with prayer may result in great success. We are living in a busy age, are always in a hurry, and are cumbered with much serving. Does it help to take time to pray? Yes, indeed. Many great things happen when God's people call upon Him. Souls are saved, burdens are lifted, power comes, revivals start, missionary enterprises gain momentum, churches make mighty strides when we pray. Prayer changes things and prayer changes people.

The secretary bird has wings and can fly. But often, we are told, when an enemy pursues him he doesn't have the sense to rise up and fly, so his enemy captures him. The Christian also has wings — the wings of prayer. At any time he can mount up upon those wings. But often, when he is in trouble, he forgets to pray. He doesn't use those wings and his troubles overcome him.

Look at the people involved in my text. They had been witnessing faithfully to the resurrection of Christ. Then troublous times came, persecution began and

they were forbidden to speak again in the name of
Jesus. And what did they do? What was their answer
to this threat? "They lifted up their voice to God with
one accord" (Acts 4:24). And "when they had prayed"
glorious things began to happen. The same things will
happen when we pray. Let us see what happened
when these wonderful people prayed.

I. They Were Filled With the Holy Spirit

They had a great task confronting them and the op-
position was fierce. They needed a greater power than
their own. They needed courage and wisdom. They
needed the power that only the Holy Spirit could give
them. That is the supreme need of God's people today.
While we know that the Holy Spirit comes into the be-
liever's heart when he is saved, he needs more — he
needs the infilling of the spirit as he faces the tasks
before him.

Why are we not continually being filled with the
Holy Spirit? It is because our lives and hearts are filled
with so many worldly things. The Holy Spirit is ready
to fill us when the need arises, but He is crowded
into a tiny corner by other things. Here is a great
dam with a mighty power plant below it and the water
above it. The machinery in the power plant is still and
it generates no power, because the water is held back.
But when the gates are opened the water flows swiftly,
the machinery begins to hum and power is generated.
And here is the human heart and life, capable of doing
great things for God, but the power is held back by our
worldliness. Oh, let us cast the world out and pray for
the Spirit to rush in and turn the wheels of our lives
and give us spiritual power!

Some zealous people tell us that they "have gotten"

the Holy Spirit, therefore the carnal nature has been slain and they have become perfect. No, that is extremism. It is not a matter of our "getting the Holy Spirit," it is rather a matter of His getting us. We are not to strive to get more of Him, but let Him have more of us. He is not a power for us to use, but we are to be persons for Him to use. To be filled with the Holy Spirit means that we are to throw out of our lives all that displeases God and let the Spirit have full possession.

It is easy to organize, to preach, to sing, but nothing will happen unless all of this is empowered by the Holy Spirit. God's power is waiting, ready to possess us and empower us. That power fell upon those early Christians when they prayed, and that is when we also can expect it. "If ye then, being evil, know how to give good gifts unto your children: how much more shall your heavenly Father give the Holy Spirit to them that ask him?" (Luke 11:13).

These men prayed, then they went out to turn the world upside down. Where did they receive the power and the courage to do this? They received it after they had prayed, for we read that "they were all filled with the Holy Spirit." Oh, weak, powerless, failing Christian, pray and power shall be thine.

II. They Found a New Courage

They were told not to speak or teach in the name of Jesus (Acts 4:18), but they "spake the word of God with boldness" (Acts 4:31). We are often timid concerning the things of God, but through prayer our timidity is overcome and we find a new courage.

Peter did not have the courage to admit to a serving girl that he knew Jesus, but on the day of Pentecost he spoke with boldness to a great multitude concerning Christ, and three thousand people were saved. His boldness came after ten days of prayer and when he became filled with the Holy Spirit. They said to Martin Luther, "You will be killed if you go up to the Diet of Worms." But he answered, "If every tile on every house in the city turned into a devil, I will still go up and take my stand." His courage was born of prayer and close communion with Christ.

A certain martyr, on the way to his death, said to his executioner, "Feel of my pulse, it is calmer than yours." His courage was born of prayer. It was said that the personal presence of Caesar made every common soldier a hero. And when we pray, the personal presence of Jesus makes us bold to stand up for Him.

We need courage today to help us stand up for our convictions. When all others around us are doing the questionable things, we must have courage to say "No." One great American statesman said, "I would rather be right than president." Don't be a fence-straddler. Get on the right side. Ask God for courage to be true always to Him and the highest and best in life. When these people of the text prayed, great boldness was theirs.

III. They Became a United People

We read that they "were of one heart and soul" (Acts 4:32). We need this spirit in our churches today. Many of our churches are torn with strife and envy and jealousy. This is a sign that they have not prayed enough. When two men kneel down and pray together, they are brought closer together. If we could get all the factions in our churches to really pray together, the divisions could be healed.

In mythology we read about Cadmus, who slew a dragon. Then he took the dragon's teeth and sowed them broadcast in a fertile field. When he returned later he found that each seed had sprung up into a giant. He was afraid of what they might do to him so he decided to employ a clever ruse to cause the giants to fight each other. He threw a stone and struck one of the giants on the ear. This giant thought that another giant had struck him, so a fight ensued. Soon all the giants were fighting each other and before long all of them were killed, while Cadmus looked on and laughed.

Our churches are full of potential spiritual giants, but Satan often sows discord among the members and they end up as spiritual pygmies, fighting one another. This gives Satan his highest joy. But when Christians really pray together, they are more likely to become of one mind in the Lord.

IV. They Had a True Sense of Stewardship

"Neither said any of them that ought of the things which he possessed was his own" (Acts 4:32). They realized that they had been bought with a price, that they had been redeemed by the precious blood of Christ, so they knew that both they and all they owned belonged to God. They were ready to put everything at His disposal.

Here is a big lesson for today's Christians. God has given us all that we have, but He asks that at least one-tenth should be returned to Him to be used for the spread of the Gospel around the world. Then the remaining nine-tenths is to be used wisely in such a way as to glorify God. Through prayer we come to realize and carry out our stewardship obligations. Consecrated people are praying people. In prayer they learn to do the Lord's will in material matters.

Every man loves someone or something better than anything else. If we love God as we should, if we have no other gods before Him, we shall want to do the will of God in all matters. But in giving only can we do His will perfectly. We can give our tithes and offerings just as He directs us in the Bible. Everyone can do that, and in prayer we learn to rightly relate ourselves to God in the matter of our material possessions.

V. They Became Attractive Christians

"Great grace was upon them" (Acts 4:33). I am sure this means that they became happy, winsome, buoyant Christians. The long-faced people, those who never smile, those who criticize continually, those who are always telling us how good they are, these people are a reproach to Christianity. Jesus was most attractive in His personality. He was so good and kind and lovable that the crowds followed Him and the little children hovered close to Him.

It was said of Socrates that he was "all beautiful within." That's what Christians ought to be. Dr. Len G. Broughton was a great preacher of another day. He was not very attractive in his physical appearance. I heard him say once, "I always look as if I am going to die in three days." On one occasion he was to preach in a certain church in Kansas City. Two women who had never seen him sat in the balcony together. When Dr. Broughton rose to speak one of them whispered, "Isn't he ugly?" But soon, with his charming manner and great gospel preaching, he made them forget about his ugliness, and then this same woman whispered, "Isn't he beautiful?"

Tradition tells us that Paul was hunchbacked and weak-eyed. But the grace of God was upon him and he must have been "all beautiful within." Just look at one scene in his life. He was on the way back to Jerusalem and stopped at Miletus to say "good-by" to the Ephesian elders. He knew that he would never see them again on this earth. He spoke to them there on the beach, and knelt down and prayed with them. Then we read that these elders wept and fell on Paul's neck and kissed him, sorrowing greatly because he had said that he would see them no more. The little hunchbacked, weak-eyed preacher must have been greatly loved, because the grace of God was upon him. This grace comes through prayer.

A little girl spent some time in a hospital where she first came to know about Jesus. On her last day there she said to a sour-faced nurse, "I have had a good time here and now I am going home. But I have learned to love Jesus so I can take my good time with me. Do you know about Jesus?" And the nurse answered, "Yes, but that's something we don't talk about." Then the little girl said, "You look so glum that I didn't think you knew Him. I didn't think anybody could be glum if they knew Jesus." We know Jesus. Are we attractive Christians?

When Moses came back from the mountain where he had been communing with God, his face was shining. And when we commune with God, we come from His presence as sweeter, gentler and more attractive Christians, and the world will feel the effect.

VI. The Place Was Shaken

Prayer shakes things. This is the secret of every great movement. One night two preachers, Paul and Silas,

spent the night in a Philippian jail. They prayed far
into the night. God heard their prayers, shook the jail
with an earthquake and released them to win the jailer
to Christ.

An American preacher once visited Spurgeon in his
great church in London. He noticed that there was no
heat in the auditorium, so he asked Spurgeon, "Don't
you have a heating plant?" Spurgeon replied by lead-
ing him down to a large basement room. In that room
four hundred men met before each service to pray for
the great pastor and the salvation of souls. Spurgeon
said, "That's our heating plant." No wonder God's
mighty power and presence were felt in every service
in that church.

A certain woman lay critically ill in Cairo, Egypt.
A friend of hers called a preacher in North Carolina.
Over the long-distance phone this preacher prayed
while the sick woman in Cairo listened in. Before long
she recovered from her illness, and when she came back
to America she went to North Carolina and thanked the
preacher for his prayers. Yes, prayer changes things
and people.

Major General O. O. Howard was a fervent Christian.
When he was out on the West Coast a group of his
friends decided to give a reception in his honor on
Wednesday night. They sent out the invitations and
even the president of the United States sent his greet-
ing. They had decided to surprise the general, but
finally they decided it would be best to tell him about
it. When they did so he said, "I'm very sorry, but I have
a previous engagement for Wednesday night." "But,"
they told him, "some of the most important people in
America will be there. You must cancel your other engagement." The general then said, "I am a Christian
and a church member. I promised the Lord when I

united with the church that I would meet Him in the prayer meeting each Wednesday night. Nothing in the world would make me break that promise." So his friends changed the reception to Thursday night. The general's influence for Christ was said to be the greatest of any man in the country during his time. He knew the secret of prayer and he received a power to shake men for God.

The captain of a small ship was taken ill while at sea. There was medicine in the medicine chest, but those on board the ship didn't know which medicine to give the captain for his particular illness. There was one hope — maybe they could send a message out and it would be picked up by a ship which had a doctor on board. So the radio operator flung out a message for help, north, east, south and west. Soon an answer came across the waves, the correct medicine was given to the captain and his life was saved. Somebody called this "a parable of prayer." But we see one difference here. The radio operator sent out a message over the air waves, hoping that someone somewhere would hear it. He did not know whether or not the message would be received. But when we pray it is not a message flung aimlessly into the air. We send it directly to God. We know there is One who will hear, and we know our cry will reach the Father's ear.

In a quiet village there lived a godly man, his wife and three boys. When his wife died suddenly he was left with the burden of bringing up the boys in the right way. Realizing his inadequacy he cried out to God for help. In one room there was an old rush-bottom chair where he often knelt to pray. The boys would sometimes peep in and see their father in prayer. But when they grew up to manhood they became prosperous and left God out of their lives. Still the faithful father kept on praying. As he later lay on his deathbed he prayed, "Lord, please let my death bring my boys to Christ."

The boys came home for the funeral. Afterward they gathered in the home to decide what should be done with the furniture. One boy suggested that it be given to the woman who had cared for their father during his last days. Then the oldest son said, "But I want that old rush-bottom chair where father always knelt to pray. I can hear his prayers now and, God helping me, I am going to answer them. I am going to be a Christian." The older boys were deeply impressed, so they all knelt around the chair and spent the afternoon in prayer, with their tears falling around the old chair. Two of them became missionaries and the other became a great Christian businessman. Yes, prayer changes things and people.

Is your heart burdened? Is life hard? Are the responsibilities too heavy for you to bear alone? Then just bring it all to Jesus in prayer. Something happened when the people of my text prayed — something will happen when you pray. So I close as I began. You can do much after you have prayed; you can do little before you pray.

3

The Man Upstairs

Matthew 6:5 - 8

One of my brothers died several years ago. He had given his heart to Christ in a revival meeting which I held in Atlanta. He did not have a college education, and he did not know much of theology, but he had learned to pray. He was sick for many months before he died. One night his wife, a fine Christian woman, went in and asked him if he was ready for bed. He replied, "I will be after I have talked to the Man upstairs." There was nothing flippant or sacrilegious in his remark. He had simply learned to look on God as a close friend.

This expression was quite often used during World War II by men who felt the great need of God's presence and help. Jesus would say, "Our Father which art in heaven." Many who had not had too much religious training, but whose complete trust was in the Lord, would say, "I want to talk to the Man upstairs." So I want to bring you a message on prayer.

I. THE PROMISES OF PRAYER
II. THE PURPOSES OF PRAYER
III. THE PEOPLE OF PRAYER

I. THE PROMISES OF PRAYER

1. *God's promise to the unbeliever.* We have been told that God hears only one prayer from a sinner, "God be merciful to me a sinner." Now this very cry is evidence that the one who prays wants to be more than a sinner — he wants his sins forgiven. So the Bible says, "Whosoever shall call upon the name of the Lord shall be saved" (Romans 10:13).

There is no limitation here. "Whosoever" includes the deepest-dyed sinner in all the world. God makes His solemn promise that all who call on Him will be saved. That call is not to be mere lip recital, but something that comes from deep in a penitent heart. So if you have never been saved, let there arise from the depths of your heart a cry to God. Ask Him to save you, ask it in the name of the Lord Jesus Christ. He will keep His promise — He will save you.

2. *God's Promises to Christians.*

(1) *Concerning forgiveness for sins.* The Christian knows he is not a perfect person. Every day there comes from his life some sinful thing in word or deed or thought. He is not happy as long as these things stand between him and God. If he loves Christ he wants "nothing between." How can the Christian get sin out? By coming to God in penitence and prayer. "If we confess our sins, he is faithful and just to forgive us our sins, and to cleanse us from all unrighteousness" (I John 1:9).

David was a man after God's own heart, but he sinned grievously. After that sin he tells us how burdened and how miserable he was. He loved God and his sin stood between him and God like a dark shadow. So we hear him praying for forgiveness. "Have mercy upon me, O God, according to thy lovingkindness: according unto the multitude of thy tender mercies blot out my transgressions. Wash me throughly from mine iniquity, and cleanse me from my sin. For I acknowledge my transgressions: and my sin is ever before me" (Psalm 51:1 - 3).

(2) *Concerning our enemies.* Jesus tells us to pray for them. This is not always easy. When other people have talked about us and hurt us and damaged our reputation, it isn't always easy to pray for them, but we should pray that God would make us willing to pray for them. We can do this when we get into right relationship to God. Jesus is telling us in Luke 6:28 to "bless them that curse you, and pray for them which despitefully use you." Only then can we find peace of mind. There is no peace for the Christian when there is something between him and someone else.

(3) *Concerning wisdom.* In this modern age we certainly need wisdom. Every day we are faced with situations and decisions which baffle us. We need the wisdom which comes from on high. And this wisdom is promised to us in James 1:5, "If any of you lack wisdom, let him ask of God, that giveth to all men liberally, and upbraideth not; and it shall be given him."

(4) *Concerning healing.* "And the prayer of faith shall save the sick, and the Lord shall raise him up; and if he have committed sins, they shall be forgiven him" (James 5:15). Any pastor who has dealt with people over the years has witnessed this many times. Often he has seen God go to work and heal someone after the doctors had given them up to die.

(5) *Concerning preachers.* There are many today who criticize the preacher instead of praying for him. Most preachers that I know are good men. They are trying to do the right thing, and are seeking the Lord's will for their lives and for the churches they serve. If

you pray for them you will be doing a good work, and you will have a part in their reward. But there is no reward, here or hereafter, for criticism.

Paul makes this appeal in II Thessalonians 3:1, 2, "Finally, brethren, pray for us, that the word of the Lord may have free course, and be glorified, even as it is with you: And that we may be delivered from unreasonable and wicked men: for all men have not faith." Yes, pray for your preacher and you will be undergirding all the work he does.

(6) *Concerning the things we need.* We are needy creatures. Each new day brings some fresh need, be it physical, mental or spiritual. Paul tells us in Philippians 4:6, to "Be careful for nothing; but in every thing by prayer and supplication with thanksgiving let your requests be made known unto God." And in Philippians 4:19 he says, "But my God shall supply all your need according to his riches in glory by Christ Jesus." And that supply is ours in answer to prayer.

Every prayer should be offered in the name of Jesus. I don't like to hear someone offer a public prayer and chop it off at the end without asking in the name of the Saviour, as we are told in John 14:13, 14, "And whatsoever ye shall ask in my name, that will I do, that the Father may be glorified in the Son. If ye shall ask any thing in my name, I will do it." Prayer is not real prayer unless it is offered in His name. This means that we are relying wholly upon the merits of Jesus and not ourselves for an answer, and that when the answer comes it will be used for His glory.

If you are sick and you pray for recovery in the name of Jesus, that is appropriate if you intend to use your good health to serve Him. But if you want to get well so you can spend your life in worldliness and sin, your prayer is an unworthy one.

My friends, God the Father loves to hear us pray — He wants to hear from us. When a girl leaves home and goes to another city, her mother wants to hear from her. She wants to hear about the girl's new job, the people she had met, the church she attends, the new clothes she has bought. Her mother grieves when the daughter neglects to write. And that's the way God feels about His children. We are dear to Him, and He loved us enough to give us His Son. He wants us to come to Him with every need, every heartache, every joy, every pleasure.

I have two sons. They are both married and they both live some distance from me. I love to hear from them and their wives and children. When a stack of mail is placed on my desk and I see a letter from one of them, I push all the other letters aside and devour that letter. God loves to hear from us. When we lift our voices in prayer, that is the sweetest sound in the world to Him.

So we see that God answers every true prayer that is offered in His name, in the right spirit, and according to His will. He always answers our prayers in the way that is best for us.

II. The Purposes of Prayer

1. *To get things from God.* Now some people would dispute this idea. They would say that prayer is nothing more than spiritual communion. They would say that we are not to ask God for anything, that we are not to use Him as a divine Santa Claus. Well, prayer does bring about spiritual fellowship and communion, but over and over God tells us to ask Him for what we need. On this earth a child does not hesitate to ask his father for what he needs and the Bible encourages the chil-

dren of God to ask the heavenly Father for what they need.

In other days when we had more time, my wife and I would go downtown window shopping. We didn't plan to buy anything, for we didn't have any money. We were just looking. And sometimes a woman will stay downtown half a day and buy nothing. Some people pray like that. They don't expect to get anything from God — they are just going through the motion of prayer. But the Bible says that real prayer is asking and seeking and knocking.

And our prayers are to be definite. When you go into a restaurant for a meal, you don't say to the waitress, "Bring me some food." You are definite about the matter. You look at the menu and you say, "Bring me the T-bone steak, medium well, tossed salad with French dressing, baked potato and coffee." When you go to the grocery store you don't say, "Let me have a basket of groceries." You say, "I want a loaf of whole wheat bread, a pound of butter, two pounds of bacon and a quart of milk." You are definite in your requests.

When someone says to me, "I want you to have dinner with me sometime," it doesn't mean anything — it's too indefinite. But when they say, "Preacher, we want you to have dinner with us Tuesday night at six-thirty," that means something. I am trying to tell you that we are definite in asking about other things and we ought to be definite in our prayers.

I have been in revival meetings where the going was hard and we needed much prayer and the power of God. A visiting preacher would come in and the pastor would call on him for prayer. He would pray around the world, telling God many things God already knew, and never thinking to beg God for the salvation of souls and for His blessings upon the meeting. We ought to be definite in our praying.

2. *To get into the right attitude toward God and man.* I have often said that prayer has a reflex action. We may not always get what we want from God, but maybe as we pray we see that it was best for us not to have it. Then we are contented to forget it. Prayer helps the one who prays in this way, even though he feels sometimes that God hasn't answered his prayers.

Now if you have anything in your heart between you and someone else, that means there is something between you and God. In prayer you see your sin, and ask God to forgive you for your wrong spirit. You then get up from your knees and everything is clear, for there is nothing between you and anyone else. If you go to your knees and pray, and get up still with the wrong feeling toward someone else in your heart, you haven't truly prayed. Prayer cleanses the heart. You can't pray rightly and keep on hating someone else. Why? Because prayer brings you close to God and when you get close to Him and catch His spirit, you can't hate enyone else.

3. *To keep us from worrying.* "Be anxious for nothing, but in every thing by prayer and supplication with thanksgiving, let your requests be made known unto God. And the peace of God, which passeth all understanding, shall keep your hearts and minds through Christ Jesus" (Philippians 4:6, 7).

Do you see what this Scripture says? Instead of worrying we are to take everything to God in prayer. Then He will give you peace that passes all understanding. Every preacher who has ever tried to do anything for the Lord has had those in his church who tried to hurt him and tear down his work. I have had my share, but God has always brought me out. I have learned to take my burden to the Lord, to thank Him for what He has done in the past and to ask for His help in the present. And I can testify that He does give a peace that no one can understand.

"This poor man cried, and the Lord heard him, and saved him out of all his troubles" (Psalm 34:6). What God did for David, He can do for you.

Dr. Walter Wilson, the physician and preacher, had a sign painted and hung by his desk, "Why pray when you can worry?" This is a bit of sarcasm, but it's just about the attitude of the average Christian. He worries instead of praying and thus misses the pathway to peace.

4. *To keep in communion with God.* When we pray faithfully we develop a sweet sense of the presence of God. He seems very near. But when we neglect to pray He seems far away. In order to feel His presence we must keep the prayer channel open.

> What a fellowship, what a joy divine,
> Leaning on the everlasting arms;
> What a blessedness, what a peace is mine,
> Leaning on the everlasting arms.

III. The People of Prayer

We have thought of the promises of prayer and the purposes of prayer, now let us think of the people of prayer. Let us look at a few examples of answered prayer.

1. *Hezekiah and answered prayer.* One day a great army of Assyrians came up and encamped against Jerusalem. Sennacherib sent an insulting letter to King Hezekiah. "Your God can't save you," he wrote, "we have destroyed other cities and you are next on the list We are going to come in and slay your people and capture your city." When Hezekiah received the letter

he didn't confer with his court officials or advisers; he went to the house of the Lord. We read that he spread the letter before the Lord and began to pray. Did God answer that prayer? I'll say He did. That night God sent His angel into the camp of the Assyrians and slew 185,000 soldiers. The victory was won because of prayer.

I like the king's idea of spreading that letter before the Lord. When difficulties arise we consult everyone else under the sun, when we ought just to bring them to God and ask His help.

2. *Peter and answered prayer.* Peter, the chief apostle, was in prison and was to be slain on the next day. But that night a group of Christians met in the house of John Mark's mother and prayed earnestly for their preacher. Yet their hearts must have been heavy, for it seemed an impossibility that Peter could get out of prison. Sixteen soldiers were guarding Peter. He was sleeping between two of them, bound to them with chains. But with a great faith in God's power to deliver, Peter slept soundly.

God heard the prayers of those faithful Christians and sent an angel down to break the chains that bound Peter and to lead him out of the prison. When Peter reached the house where the believers were praying, they were amazed that their prayers had been answered. God had answered in such a marvelous way it seemed too good to be true.

In Bristol, England, a godly man's heart went out to the poor orphan children around him. In prayer he asked God to give him a home where he could take care of these children. God answered that prayer and George Muller began a remarkable career unequalled by any other man. During his lifetime he took care of more than two thousand children and raised more than

seven million dollars. He never asked anyone for
money or anything that he needed; he just told God
about it. And God put it into the hearts of good people
all over the country to supply every need. Every building that was erected, every meal that was supplied,
the salaries of all the workers, all came in without one
single collection by Muller. And besides caring for
these children, he supported hundreds of missionaries,
gave away thousands of Bibles, and established many
schools for poor children. All of his many good works
were the result of prayer.

Why are we so poor in the things that are really
worthwhile? It must be because our prayer lives are so
poor. God has all that we need and we can come with
the golden key of prayer and open the doors of His
heavenly treasure and have every need supplied. But
remember there is a condition here. We can't live
as we please and ask God to give us something, and
expect to receive it. Here is the secret in John 15:7,
"If ye abide in me, and my words abide in you, ye shall
ask what ye will, and it shall be done unto you." We
must live in Christ and close to Him every day, and
then He will keep His promise. You can't live a careless, indifferent, stingy life and expect God to pour out
His blessings upon you.

At the end of the Civil War a southern man's slaves
had all been set free. But he had one servant whom he
loved and who was devoted to him. He called him in
and said, "Sam, if you will stay with me, and if you will
care for me, I'll see that you are cared for after I am
gone." Sam loved his former master and agreed to stay
with him. He did stay with him and care for him until
the old man died. Then Sam mowed lawns, chopped
wood and ran errands until he was too old to work very

much. He lived in a poor little shack and could hardly get enough to eat.

One day a man said to him, "Sam, your old master told me that he put $5,000 in the bank for you. Go down and get what you need." So the next morning Sam went down to the bank. He shuffled up to the teller's window and said, "Did Marse Tom leave some money for me in this here bank?" "Yes," said the teller, "he left $5,000 here for you." "How can I git it?" Sam asked. The teller knew Sam couldn't write, so he said, "I'll make out a check for the amount you want, then you make your mark on the check and I'll give you the money." "Can I have as much as fifty cents?" the old man asked. "Yes," answered the teller, "you can get any amount up to $5,000." "Then just make out the check for fifty cents," Sam said. The check was made out, Sam put his cross-mark on it and the teller gave him a shining half dollar. Then Sam went out and bought a sack of meal, went back to his poor little shack and left $4,999.50 in the bank.

Isn't it that way with most of us? We know that our heavenly Father has all that we need. Then He tells us that we have only to ask for it and it will be given to us. But we go on living in physical, mental and spiritual poverty. "We have not, because we ask not." May God help us to make a good connection with the God of heaven and always to keep the channel open between us and God.

4

How Prayer Helps in the Christian Life

James 5:16 - 20

A group of preachers were on a train on the way to a convention. They talked about many things, and finally the discussion came around to the needs in a preacher's life. Many needs were spoken of and finally one older preacher who had lived a long and useful life for the Lord said, "Our greatest failure is that we do not spend more time upon our knees." If you will search your own experience, I think that you will find this is true of your own life also. Not one of us prays enough. We forfeit many hours of peace and we sacrifice many needed blessings because of our lack of prayer. We carry many unnecessary burdens because we do not take them to the Lord in prayer. Let's talk about prayer and how it helps in the Christian life.

I. FOUR THOUGHTS ABOUT PRAYER

1. *Prayer is a prelude to salvation.* "For whosoever shall call upon the name of the Lord shall be saved" (Romans 10:13). All those who have come to Christ have called upon Him in some way. You may not have prayed a very eloquent prayer, you may not have

known just what to say, but you did cry out to Him for salvation.

After Paul met Christ on the Damascus road, he was carried into the city where for three days his eyes were blinded. And what was he doing all of this time? He was praying. God told Ananias to carry a message to Paul. He told him that he would find Paul praying. Surely he must have been pleading for God to forgive all of his sins.

The Pharisee and the publican went to church. The Pharisee boasted to the Lord of his good character and good deeds. The publican beat upon his breast and cried out, "God be merciful to me, a sinner." And Jesus tells us that the publican "went down to his house justified rather than the other." No man who has ever called upon Christ for salvation has been turned down. That cry may not be audible to the human ear, but God hears that cry and God saves the sinner.

2. *Prayer is necessary for Christian growth.* As the tree needs roots, so does the Christian need prayer. Prayer is the foundation of the Christian life. Paul tells Christians to "pray without ceasing." This does not mean that you will always be speaking certain words to God, but it does mean that you will live in the atmosphere of prayer. You will live so close to God that at any moment you can reach out and touch Him through your prayer.

We ought to pray in the spirit of thanksgiving. "In every thing give thanks: for this is the will of God in Christ Jesus concerning you" (I Thessalonians 5:18). Each night as you look back over the day, you can see how God's hand has been upon you. You may have been in many dangerous places, but God has delivered you. However, this Scripture says that we are to give thanks to God "in every thing." Even when the waves of trouble sweep over us, we are to give thanks to God. Do you have a nice family? Do you have good health? Do you have a church that you love? As you think of these things, you ought to say, "God has been good to me." We take the blessings of life as a matter of fact, but there ought to be time every day when we pray in the spirit of thanksgiving.

Then we ought to pray in the spirit of penitence. We sin every day; the devil gets in his work every day. So every day we ought to ask God for forgiveness. If a man never prays, it is because he does not recognize the fact that he is a sinner. "There is not a just man upon the earth, who doeth good and sinneth not." When we were sinners we came to Christ and He forgave the damning sin of our lives. But since we still sin every day, we must come to Him for daily cleansing.

3. *We do not pray enough.* The Bible says, "Ye have not because ye ask not." We do not pray enough for ourselves. We go through life fretting, worrying, carrying many burdens. The song says, "Take your burden to the Lord and leave it there." We take our burdens to the Lord, but we do not leave them there. We continue to labor beneath their load. This simply means that we need to pray more for ourselves.

Then we don't pray enough for others. What a blessing it is to my own heart when I receive a letter from some great saint of God, telling me that he is praying for me. On one occasion when the people requested Samuel to pray for them, he said, "God forbid that I should sin against the Lord by not praying for you" (I Samuel 12:23). There are so many people around us who have so many needs that we really sin against them when we don't pray for them.

4. *God answers prayer.* I can certainly testify that He has answered my prayers. "Call unto me, and I

will answer thee, and shew thee great and mighty things, which thou knowest not" (Jeremiah 33:3).

II. How Prayer Helps in the Christian Life

1. *Prayer helps in the time of trouble.* Trouble is the universal lot of us all. The sun may shine brightly for awhile, but we know that trouble will eventually come, and prayer will sustain us in the hour of trouble.

It is certainly good to have God's help in time of need. "Man's extremity is God's opportunity." But why do we wait for the grim hour of trouble to come upon us before we pray? We need to live daily in the atmosphere of prayer. Then when trouble comes, we will find it easier to pray, because we have already opened up a channel between us and God.

2. *Prayer helps in the time of sorrow.* What would we do in time of sorrow if we could not look up into God's face and pour out our hearts to Him? I have seen people who cried out in despair when sorrow came. I have seen others who had the peace of God written in their faces when sorrow fell upon them. They had that peace because they had been alone with God. Some years ago I knew a fine Christian man. When he was upon his deathbed he called the family around him, assured them that all was well with him, and prayed for them, commending them to God's grace. I could tell a difference at the funeral. These people had learned what to do in time of sorrow. Comfort and strength was theirs. Surely we need to pray in time of sorrow.

3. *Prayer helps us to find God's will for our lives.* I believe that God has a will for every life, and that will can be found through prayer and full surrender. You have heard the old joke about the preacher who

was called to a new church, and how he said to his wife, "You pack up while I pray about this call." That is not true of the majority of preachers. The average preacher wants to know the will of God for his life. One such preacher told me that he had been called to a new field. He did not want to leave the church where he was serving, but he said this in a letter, "It breaks my heart to go, but I am under orders from the Lord." Yes, you can find God's plan for your life in prayer.

4. *Prayer helps us to overcome temptation.* What do so many of us do when temptation comes? We embrace it instead of flying to God in prayer. Like David of old, we look upon the sin and soon we are indulging in it. The Bible gives us a guarantee of overcoming power. "There hath no temptation taken you but such as is common to man: but God is faithful, who will not suffer you to be tempted above that ye are able; but will with the temptation also make a way to escape, that ye may be able to bear it" (I Corinthians 10:13).

5. *Prayer helps us to get better acquainted with Jesus.* When you have a good friend, you want to talk to him. The more you talk with him, the better do you become acquainted with him. Jesus is the best Friend man ever had. You become better acquainted with Him through intimate communion with Him.

6. *Prayer helps us to give good service to Christ.* The great men of the Bible were great because of prayer and close communion with God. Martin Luther said, "I have so much to do that I could never accomplish it if I did not spend at least two hours each day in prayer." The time spent in prayer is never wasted. You can do much more after you pray, than if you had never prayed at all. The Sunday school teacher should pray before going to her class. The singer should pray before every song. The preacher should surely pray before

he mounts the pulpit. Do you feel that you are a weak vessel? Do you feel that you are doing little for God? Then pray about it. Here is a verse for you. "But they that wait upon the Lord shall renew their strength; they shall mount up with wings as eagles; they shall run, and not be weary; and they shall walk, and not faint" (Isaiah 40:31). Won't you pray more that God will use you as a vessel to live for Him and win others to Him? Prayer is the greatest force in any Christian life.

> The camel, at the close of day,
> Kneels down upon the sandy plain
> To have his burden lifted off
> > And rest to gain.

> My soul, thou, too, shouldst to thy knees
> When daylight draweth to a close,
> And let the Master lift the load
> > And grant repose.

> Else how canst thou tomorrow meet
> With all tomorrow's work to do,
> If thou thy burden all the night
> > Dost carry through?

> The camel kneels at break of day
> To have his guide replace his load,
> Then rises up anew to take
> > The desert road.

> So thou shouldst kneel at morning's dawn
> That God may give thee daily care,
> Assured that He no load too great
> > Will make thee bear.

5

Power in Prayer

John 15:7

We live in an age of tremendous power. We go to Niagara Falls or to some of the great dams in the west and we think of how power goes out to light great cities and turn the wheels of commerce. This is electric power. We remember that in 1945 a destructive bomb was dropped on Hiroshima, killing thousands of people. This is atomic power. We think of how that today a small piece of matter can be placed on a ship and that ship can go around the world on that power. That is nuclear power. At Cape Kennedy a man is shot up into space and he makes several orbits around the world. That is rocket power. We are told that there are installations in America where a bomb can be launched to fly thousands of miles into the heart of Russia. That is missile power.

But the Christian's greatest available power is the power of prayer. The text says, "If ye abide in me, and my words abide in you, ye shall ask what ye will, and it shall be done unto you." And John 14:14 says, "If ye shall ask any thing in my name, I will do it." But we don't avail ourselves of this power simply by asking. There must be a clean heart and a pure life behind the prayer. There must be a surrendered will. There must be a request according to His will. The prayer must be in the name of Jesus, and it all must be for God's glory.

I. Why Should We Pray?

1. *Because Jesus set the example.* Every true Christian wants to be like Jesus. If that is true, the Christian must pray much. Jesus prayed all the way from the cradle to the grave. He taught His disciples to pray. I think His favorite place of prayer must have been under the old olive trees in the garden of Gethsemane. On the night before the crucifixion Judas wanted to find Him and turn Him over to His enemies. He knew where to find Him. He went to the place of prayer, and led the mob to Gethsemane.

Look at the type of prayers He offered. He prayed always for others. He prayed that His works and His words might glorify God. Even on the cross, bleeding His life away, His prayer was for others. How different are our prayers. They consist mostly of "give me this and give me that." A certain mother said to her little girl, "You didn't say your prayers last night." And the little girl replied, "But I didn't want anything." That is so much like us. We don't stop to pray unless there is some great need in our lives.

Jesus prayed for His enemies as well as His friends. All along the way He is praying for His disciples, those who followed Him then and those who follow Him now. In His high-priestly prayer in John 17 He prayed for all of them who would, in years to come, believe on Him. He is still praying for us in heaven. But look at Him on the cross. He is suffering all the agonies of hell. Did He think of Himself, did He pray for Himself, did He pronounce a curse on those who were killing Him? No, He prayed for them, "Father, forgive them; for they know not what they do" (Luke 23:34).

Can you pray like that? Can you say, "Father, they have wronged me, but please forgive them even as I forgave them?" If someone speaks out against you or accuses you wrongfully, can you pray for him? "But I say unto you, Love your enemies, bless them that curse you, do good to them that hate you, and pray for them which despitefully use you, and persecute you" (Matthew 5:44). Yes, Jesus has set the example for us in prayer.

2. *Because there is a devil.* He is a person of mighty cunning and power. He besets the pathway of every Christian, seeking to trip him and hurt his influence for Christ. The Bible refers to him as a "roaring lion, seeking whom he may devour" (I Peter 5:8). He delights to bring alluring temptations before us, then he rejoices when we fall. There is only one way to overcome him. We must pray against him. The Bible says, "Resist the devil, and he will flee from you" (James 4:7). We are not to flirt with him, are not to listen to him, are not to embrace him, but are to resist him.

> Take the name of Jesus ever
> As a shield from every snare;
> If temptations round you gather,
> Breathe that holy name in prayer.

The devil tempts us daily. He uses every device under the sun to bring us down. When he comes at us we are not to plunge into sin. We are to stop and think and, most of all, to pray. The devil is strong, but God is stronger. God will help us for He will provide a way to escape. Prayer and sin do not go together. When we pray we can defeat the devil, for "Satan trembles when he sees the weakest saint upon his knees."

3. *Because prayer is God's way for us to obtain His blessings.* Here is a little child who needs a pair of shoes. How does he get them? He asks his father for them. Our heavenly Father has all that we need and He invites us, yea, He urges us to come and ask Him for these things. "Ask, and it shall be given you; seek, and ye shall find; knock, and it shall be opened unto you" (Matthew 7:7).

4. *Because our souls grow when we pray.* We want to grow physically and mentally, why not spiritually? The man who prays will grow in grace. I visited in a home where there was a thirty year old "child." He had grown physically, he had the body of a man, but he had the mind of a baby. He could neither read nor write, nor could he speak plainly. His father looked on him with affection, but I am sure his heart ached because his son had not grown mentally. But let me tell you of a sadder thing. God saves a person and the years go by. That person grows physically, mentally, socially and financially, but there is not an inch of spiritual growth. The heart of God must be heavy when He looks upon such a person. The main reason for lack of growth is lack of prayer. Prayer keeps a Christian in close communion with God and promotes Christian growth. We need the power of the Holy Spirit in our lives. We need to feel His presence, to respond to His guidance. He is in the heart of all believers, but some have more power than others. Why? Because they are living close to God in prayer. Jesus promised the Holy Spirit to those who prayed for His power in their lives. Are you satisfied with your Christian growth? Do you pray as much as you should?

II. How Should We Pray?

1. *We should pray submissively.* A human father does not respond to the plea of a disobedient child. Neither does our heavenly Father. If God is calling you to do a certain thing and you refuse, you need not expect an answer to your prayers. It is when we are abiding in Him, when we are walking with Him, when we are carrying out all of His wishes, that He answers our prayers.

He may not call you to be a missionary or a preacher or to occupy some high public position. But every Christian is called to serve Him. He may be calling you to some place of service in the church. It may be a very obscure place, but if God calls you, that is His place for you. It is far better to be in some small place with God by your side than in the limelight alone.

He may be calling you to give of your time, your talent, your tithe. As long as you withhold these things from God, your prayers will go unanswered. He may be calling you to go next door and witness to that neighbor as to the saving grace of Christ. He may be calling you to visit that shut-in and bring a little sunshine into his dreary life. Go and do His bidding, then you'll have a right to ask God for the things you need.

Some time ago a man told me that he prayed every day. Yet that man never goes to the house of the Lord and never gives a cent of money to the cause of Christ. He is thus being disobedient to the Lord. I wonder if his prayers mean very much. We should pray submissively. Jesus set the example for us in the garden of Gethsemane when He prayed, "Not my will, but thine be done." If we pray submissively we will pray within the will of God.

2. *We are to pray thankfully.* Oh, we have so many things to be thankful for! All of life and its blessings and all of the future life and its joys are ours because of the love and goodness of God. We should live in the atmosphere of gratitude, looking up always to Him who is the giver of every good and perfect gift. Paul tells us to make our requests known unto God "with thanksgiving." The thoughtful heart is the thankful heart. The right kind of thinking leads to thanking.

When I was a seminary student I heard Dr. M. E. Dodd, for many years pastor of the First Baptist Church of Shreveport, preach on prayer. He gave his own personal formula for prayer. He said that as he came to pray, he would first shut his eyes, then he would try to think about the kind of Father God is. Soon he would be counting the blessings God had given him and in a few minutes he said he would be in the right attitude to look into God's face and pour out his heart to Him. This simply means that he was praying thankfully.

3. *We are to pray expectantly.* Jesus said that we could move mountains if we had faith as large as a mustard seed. You have heard the story of the dear old woman whose view from her window was obstructed by a mountain. Then she heard about this Scripture and she decided to ask God to move the mountain. So one night she put this plea in her prayer. She asked God to move the mountain. The next morning she looked out of the window and the mountain was still there, whereupon she exclaimed, "There it is, just as I expected."

Jesus said that we are to ask "believing," we are to ask "in faith." He keeps His promise. As we pray we must have faith, believing that God will answer in the way that is always best for us.

4. *We are to pray perseveringly.* Paul said that we are to "pray without ceasing." Of course that doesn't mean that we are to go around mumbling some petition to God all the time. But it does mean that we are to live in the atmosphere of prayer, so that at any time we can reach out and touch the hem of His garment as we pray. I think it means also that we are to keep on praying. God doesn't always say "Yes" the first time we ask Him for something. Maybe He delays the answer until we are better fitted to receive it. So we are to keep on praying, as long as we measure up to His requirements and as long as it is according to His will.

Jacob didn't receive the answer the first hour as he wrestled with the angel, who was evidently the Old Testament manifestation of Christ. But he kept on wrestling until finally he cried out, "I will not let thee go, except thou bless me" (Genesis 32:26). The blessing came and with it the Lord's touch upon Jacob's thigh. From that hour Jacob was a different man. He "limped upon his thigh," but he was limping to glory. He persevered in prayer. Oh, that we might learn that lesson.

Even Jesus Himself did not receive the answer the first time He prayed in Gethsemane. Three times He prayed in agony and heaviness and blood. Then the answer came and He could say, "Not my will, but thine be done. I will drink the cup of separation and suffering down to the last dregs." The Bible tells us that "the effectual fervent prayer of a righteous man availeth much," not the lukewarm prayer.

III. THREE CONDITIONS GOVERNING PRAYER

1. *The one who prays must have a vital connection with God.* He must have been born again and he must

be connected with God through the ties of grace and faith. God has not promised His blessings and power to the sinner, the man who has no connection with Him.

Remember the Bible story of Elijah and the prophets of Baal? An altar had been built on Mt. Carmel. The wood was there for the fire. The prophets and Elijah were to pray to their respective Gods. The one who sent the fire down upon the altar was to be declared the true God. Elijah graciously gave the prophets of Baal the first opportunity. Surely he knew what he was doing; he knew the true God. Well, the prophets prayed for many hours but their god didn't hear, the fire didn't fall. Then Elijah began to mock them, "Maybe your god is asleep or maybe he has gone on a journey," he said. And in their desperation they pulled out their swords and lances and cut themselves until the blood gushed out. They hoped that Baal would see that blood and answer their prayers, but nothing happened.

Then Elijah said, "Come near and let me show you what the real God can do." So he poured water all over the altar and all around the altar, doing this three times. Surely no fire can burn that wood now. But listen to old faithful, faith-filled Elijah. He called upon God beseeching Him to show His power so that the people might know that He was the true God. And God answered that simple prayer. The fire fell and consumed the sacrifice and all the wood and all the water. It was such a mighty manifestation of God's power that the people fell on their faces and cried out, "The Lord He is God, the Lord He is God." Now why was Elijah's simple prayer answered and not the desperate pleas of the prophets of Baal? It was because Elijah had a vital connection with God and the prophets prayed only into the empty air. They had no vital connection with Him who answers prayer.

On a hillside nearby is a tank of water and here on the ground is some pipe, lying idle. You will never get any water through that pipe until it is connected with the source of water. In heaven is God, with all the blessings He has for us. And here is a man with no connection with God, therefore he cannot expect to receive His blessings. But a Christian, a child of God, is vitally connected with God. He can pray, and His prayers will bring the blessings down.

2. *The channel of life must be pure.* David said, "If I regard iniquity in my heart, the Lord will not hear me." If there is sin in our lives, our prayers will not go higher than our heads.

I am sure this has happened to many of us. As we prayed God showed us something wrong in our lives. Maybe it was a secret sin, maybe it was an act of disobedience toward God; maybe it was some animosity or bad feeling that we had toward someone else. We knew right then that our prayer would not be answered. So we cried out to the Lord, confessing our sin and asking Him to help us get it out of our hearts. Then, with the channel open, we could communicate with God.

When I was a boy we had a wonderful well of pure water at our home. Many people who drank from that well would exclaim, "My, what fine water." It was always cold and sweet and good to the taste, but when winter came we would close up the well and drink the water that came from the faucet. Then when spring rolled around my father would employ a well-digger and his assistant to clean out the well. This was always an exciting time for me as a little boy. The well-digger would go down into the dark hole with a big wooden bucket. His assistant handled the windlass at the top of the well. The man in the well would fill the big bucket with the old stale water and all the impure things he found down there, and his assistant would draw them to the top and pour them out. Soon the well would be cleaned of all of its impurities and the pure water would be flowing again, clean and good and cold.

We must do something like that if our prayers are to be answered. We must go down deep into our lives and clear out all the sin, the malice, the hatred, the impurities. Only then can we pray rightly, only then can we expect the blessings to flow.

3. *The prayer must be for God's glory.* Jesus emphasized the fact that we are to ask for blessings in His name. You say, "That's fine, I'll ask Him for a Cadillac and a new home and a million dollars." But when we ask in His name that does away with foolish requests. We come to ask for those things that will glorify Him and not for something that would please our own selfish selves.

There are some people who do not pray now, but the Bible tells us that there will come a time when they will pray with all the fervor of their souls. They go on now without God and without hope. But in Revelation 6: 16 we read that in that awful day they shall cry out for the rocks and the mountains to fall on them and hide them from the wrath of the Lamb. They will pray but their prayers will be too late. Judgment is coming. If you are not ready, if you have not prayed the sinner's prayer "God be merciful to me a sinner," I advise you to start praying right now.

Some of you remember how you liked to sit down by your mother and father and talk things over with them. They are gone now — you can't talk to them face to face — but there is One who never dies. He is always by your side, and He wants you to talk things over with Him. You can take all your troubles to Him, for He cares for you.

Some years ago an evangelist was holding a revival in a southern town. At the close of the service one night he invited all those who were burdened for unsaved loved ones to come up and tell him about it, so that he could join them in prayer for the salvation of these who didn't know Christ. One woman came up to tell him that her husband, a railroad engineer, was unsaved. The preacher asked her if she had ever spent a night in prayer for him. She said that she had never thought of doing that. Then the preacher said, "I don't think any preacher will ever get your husband heavy on his heart unless you are willing to spend a night in prayer for him." This cut her very deeply. She went home and put the baby in bed, then she went into the living room, dropped down by the sofa and began to pray for her husband.

He was down at the railroad roundhouse, ready to take his engine out on his run. Then a strange feeling came to him, a feeling that for some reason he ought to go home. He tried to shake off that feeling but it came back again. Finally he called in someone to take his place, and he rushed home. When he found his wife sobbing out her heart to God he said, "What's the matter? Is there something wrong with the baby?" "No," she replied, "but there is something wrong with you. You are lost and I have been praying for your salvation. I have promised God that I would not sleep nor eat until, in some way, I could know that you were going to be saved." I do not need to tell you that he was saved that night, and that on the next Sunday he made a public profession of his faith and joined the church. Again prayer had been answered.

Oh, the marvelous, mighty power of prayer! Oh, the wonderful prayer promises in the Word of God! Oh, how gloriously God has answered our prayers in the past! Why don't we claim these promises and this power for our lives today?

6

A Little Talk with Jesus

Luke 11:9, 10

The children have a song which says, "A little talk with Jesus makes it right, all right." That is what prayer is, just talking to Jesus. And how we do need to pray today! We live in a complex age and a confused world. We face decisions and we carry responsibilities which probably no generation has ever faced. Yet to many people prayer is a lost art. We stumble along life's way, trying to bear our burdens alone, trying to find the right path to walk, when all the time God is just waiting for us to call upon Him, that He might put all of His resources at our disposal.

The most serious indictment that can be brought against Christians today is that they don't pray enough. We worry, we fret, we fume, we fuss, we do not pray as we should. God says, "Call unto me," but we turn our backs on Him and call on our petty resources. No wonder we are such halting, limping, weak Christians.

The great men of the Bible were men of prayer. They rightly felt that they could not get along without constant communion with God. Moses had a big job — God commissioned him to lead more than two million people out of the slavery of Egypt into the freedom of the Promised Land. He confessed his weakness — his inability to do the job — but God assured him that He would be with him all the way. And over and over Moses reminded God of that promise, calling on Him in prayer to help him and guide him as the problems of the journey beset him.

And think of what a man of prayer David was. Most of the psalms that he wrote were fervent prayers to the Almighty. If he was not praying he was testifying to the way in which God did answer his prayers.

Elijah prayed and God shut up the heavens and held back the rain for more than three years. He prayed again and God sent the rain to refresh the earth. John the Baptist prayed in the wilderness and came forth as a giant for God. Peter and the little handful of believers prayed for ten days, and the power of the Holy Spirit fell and three thousand were saved in a day. Paul was a praying man. From the moment he met Christ on the Damascus Road until he died, he never let go of God. And Jesus, God's own Son, kept in constant touch with God by praying from the cradle to the grave.

I. THE OBLIGATION TO PRAY

II. THE OBSERVANCE OF PRAYER

III. THE OPPORTUNITIES TO PRAY

I. THE OBLIGATION TO PRAY

1. *We owe it to ourselves.* God loves His children and wants them to have some of His bountiful blessings from above. But the receiving of these blessings is often dependent upon our asking for them. "Ye have not because ye ask not," says the Word of God. We are often in the predicament of the prodigal son when he found himself in the pigpen. He said, "My father's

servants have bread enough and to spare, and I perish with hunger." Our heavenly Father has all we shall ever need, but we perish because we do not ask for it.

We cheat ourselves when we do not pray. Paul knew of God's great supply and he said, "My God shall supply all your need according to his riches in glory by Christ Jesus" (Philippians 4:19). Those riches are ours through prayer.

2. *We owe it to others.* In James 5:16 we are told to "pray one for another." How I do thank God for those in many places who tell me that they pray for me. I just don't feel I could go on if I didn't have someone praying for me. I have felt the power of those prayers on many occasions. We owe it to many people to pray for them. Our missionaries on the foreign field tell us that their greatest need is for us to pray for them. Nothing gives a Christian worker more comfort and courage than to receive a letter saying, "I am praying for you."

Samuel was a man of prayer. The people had sinned against God and He had punished them for their sin. Then they trembled before the Lord and begged Samuel to pray for them. Samuel replied in I Samuel 12:23, "God forbid that I should sin against the Lord in ceasing to pray for you." He not only felt an obligation to pray for others, he also felt that he would be sinning against God if he didn't pray for others.

There are lost souls all around us. We are to pray for them, that the Holy Spirit might convict them of their lost condition and point them to Jesus. There are your children growing up around you. They are going to face many problems in this sinful world. Every day they should be the burden of your prayers. Your church needs your prayers, your pastor needs your prayers. Our country's leaders need your prayers. We are admonished to pray for them. There are burdened hearts around you — so many people who need your prayers.

When I was a student in the seminary in Texas, I served as pastor of two half-time churches. I would go out to these churches on Saturday and spend two nights in the homes of the members, coming back on Monday. As bedtime would approach in these homes I would always kneel with the family in prayer. But before our prayer the parents in the home would tell me about their grown sons and daughters who had moved to other cities and states. I would then include them in the prayer. I am sure that those sons and daughters felt the power of these prayers of mine and of those who loved them. Many a prodigal has been brought home, many a wanderer turned away from sin by the prayers of a loving family. Yes, we owe it to others to pray.

3. *We owe it to God.* I have seen hogs under an apple tree, eating apples, but they never looked up to see where the apples came from. We don't expect anything else from a hog. But there are too many people like that. They eat and drink and use the blessings of God, and never look up into His face to say, "Thank You, Lord."

Shakespeare said, "How sharper than a serpent's tooth it is to have a thankless child." If a child's ingratitude hurts his father, how much more does our ingratitude hurt the heart of God. Jesus was evidently greatly disappointed when, after He had cleansed ten men of the dread disease of leprosy, only one came back to thank Him.

And, oh, how much we do need to thank God for His wonderful salvation. We were condemned, we were doomed, we were bound for hell. But in His gracious mercy He saved us "by the washing of regeneration, and renewing of the Holy Spirit." Surely we ought to thank Him now for saving us and surely we'll want to thank Him throughout eternity for it.

II. The Observance of Prayer

1. *We are to pray with clean hearts.* We can't reach God when our hearts are filled with sin. As a cloud on a sunny day comes between us and the sun, so does sin come between us and God. David knew God and he knew how sin separated one from God, so he said, "If I regard iniquity in my heart, the Lord will not hear me" (Psalm 66:18). The ancient Jew at Passover time, wanting to draw close to God, cleansed his heart and his house and said, "Lord, if there is sin in my household, it is against my will." Jesus said that before making an offering to God, we should make things right with our brother. Our prayers go no higher than our heads when our hearts are filled with sin. When we get the world out, we can get up to God.

A man goes into a beautiful cathedral to worship. There are aids to worship all around him, windows of beautiful glass, pictures that point to God, everything. But he cannot worship at his best, because the doors are open and the raucous sounds of the marketplace drown out the voice of the spiritual. No, we are not able to pray aright until we shut the world out.

A certain prosperous man was able to give his son anything. Now the boy wanted a bicycle but he did not dare ask for it. His school grades were very low and he knew there was no use to ask for the bicycle until he brought his grades up. There are times when we dare not ask God for anything. Our lives are not right — our grades are too low. We must make things right with God and then we have the right to ask Him for needed things.

I have often stood by the sickbed of some church member who was living a careless, indifferent, worldly life. I would want to offer a prayer and the patient would often say, "Preacher, please pray for me." But I would wonder on what basis I could offer that prayer. Could I call God's attention to the fine life he had been living and ask God to spare him because of that life? Could I base my prayer on the hope that maybe in the future he would live a better life? No, I could base my prayer only on the mercy and goodness and grace of God. But if men would come to God, asking forgiveness for sin and cleansing, then surely their prayers would be more effective.

2. *We are to pray with grateful hearts.* Our requests are to be made "with thanksgiving." In the book, *Uncle Tom's Cabin,* the slaves were complaining of their hard lot in life. But Uncle Tom, Christian that he was, said, "But think on the mercies, think on the mercies." And as we look all around us at the mercies and blessings of God, surely we are bound to pray gratefully.

3. *We are to pray with earnestness.* Our prayers are not to be mere "mouthings," the simple saying of words. We are to feel them, and we are to pray from the depths of our souls. It is the "effectual, fervent" prayer which reaches the heart of God.

4. *We are to pray with expectancy.* In Isaiah 65:24 God says, "Before they call, I will answer; and while they are yet speaking, I will hear." Mark 11:24 says, "What things soever ye desire, when ye pray, believe that ye receive them." Mark 9:23 says, "If thou canst believe, all things are possible to him that believeth." Oh, what wonderful promises made by a loving Father! I went through college and seminary, with a wife and

two children, basing my hope and help on these verses, often singing the little chorus:

> Only believe, only · believe,
> All things are possible,
> Only believe.

At a mission station in India an orphan girl named Kara was saved. She was to be sold in slavery, but the missionaries, hoping to save her from such a life, wanted to keep her in the mission station. They had no money for her support but one of the missionaries said, "Kara, you pray and we'll pray and I believe God will make it possible for us to take you in." Kara went back home and that very day the missionary received a check from an unexpected source. The next morning he started out to see Kara and to tell her of his good fortune, but he met Kara coming toward the mission station. She said, "We were both praying and I felt that God was going to answer, so I started out." She had prayed with expectancy.

5. *We are to pray with hearts seeking wisdom.* James 1:5 says: "If any of you lack wisdom, let him ask of God, that giveth to all men liberally, and upbraideth not; and it shall be given them." The highest wisdom in this world is to know the will of God. We find that wisdom and that will when we pray.

6. *We are to pray with definite requests.* When a child needs something he doesn't approach his father and ask in generalities. He tells his father just what he needs. And that is the way we should approach God. We are to consult Him in definite terms about every phase of life.

III. The Opportunities to Pray

1. *We should have a definite time and place.* Every Christian, every day, should have some time set aside

for prayer. It is good to have the same time each day, making your prayer time as definitely a part of your daily routine as you do your meals. And I think it would be good to have a spot where you get away from all the world and where you meet God face to face. Such a place becomes a sacred spot, a piece of holy ground in a sinful world.

2. *Every family should have a "family altar."* Private prayer is good and necessary, nothing else can take its place. But there should be a set time in every home when the entire family comes together to read God's Word and to pray. That time may come at night before the family retires or it may be at the breakfast table each morning, or at some other period.

A certain man said to the preacher who was to conduct his little girl's funeral, "The thing that breaks my heart is to remember that my little girl never heard a prayer in her father's home or from her father's lips."

Set up a family altar in your home. The children will never be able to get away from that scene, they'll never be able to forget it. Many a wayward man and woman have been brought back to God by remembering the earnest prayers of a father and mother in a Christian home.

3. *We are to pray "without ceasing."* Of course, this doesn't mean that we are to be fanatics — we are not to quit everything else and go around mumbling our prayers. But we are to live in the atmosphere of prayer. We are to live so close to Jesus that we can reach out and touch Him at any time.

And, if at any time, day or night, there arises in your heart and mind an impulse toward God, that impulse should not be stifled. Right then we should turn to God in prayer, "unuttered or expressed, the motion of a hidden fire that trembles in the breast."

The trouble with too many of us is that we wait until we are in distress before we begin to pray. One of our chaplains said that on the field of battle he often heard wounded men cry out, "O God," who never used that name back in the barracks except in profanity.

A little girl went to church one day with her mother. The pastor called on one of his deacons to pray. The deacon had a booming voice and his prayer seemed to shake the very rafters, it was so loud. At the close of his prayer the little girl whispered to her mother, "Mother, if he lived closer to God, he wouldn't have to talk so loudly, would he?" Yes, we all need to live so close that we can touch His hand in prayer.

Some years ago a young man, tiring of his mother's piety and restraint, decided to leave home. Before he left his mother put her hands on his shoulders and said, "Son, I'll always be here praying for you. And if there ever comes a time when the burden of life is too heavy and you don't know where to turn, just call upon your mother's God and He will surely answer." The boy went to the big city to live. He was free now to do anything he wished, and soon he fell into sin. The days passed and sin lost its pleasure for him. In a fit of deep depression, as he sat in a small hotel room, he decided to end it all by suicide. But on the table he saw a Bible and he picked it up and read a few verses. Then he seemed to hear his mother's voice, saying, "Son, when you don't know where to turn, when life's burden becomes too heavy, call on your mother's God and He will surely answer." In a few seconds he was on his knees, confessing his sin and crying to God for salvation. The Lord wondrously saved him and he decided to go home and surprise his mother with the good news.

When he reached home his mother saw him coming

up the walk and ran out to meet him. She threw her arms around his neck and said, "I know why you've come home, son. You have called upon your mother's God and He has saved you." The boy acknowledged that it was true, that God had saved him, and they rejoiced together. That young man was Dr. R. A. Torrey, who later became one of America's greatest evangelists and Bible scholars. He had prayed and God had answered.

There is power in prayer. May we all come to know anew that if we call upon God in the name of Jesus Christ, He will surely answer in the best way.

7

Prayer for Revival

Acts 1:12 - 14

The most important thing in a revival is prayer. You can have everything else, but without prayer there will be no revival. You can advertise a meeting until everyone knows about it. You can have a great choir singing heavenly music. You can raise huge sums of money. You can have overflow crowds. You can have great gospel preaching. But all of these things, as fine as they are, will not bring a revival. It must be prayed down from heaven, not worked up from earth.

I. THE MASTER'S EXAMPLE IN PRAYER

Before deciding on any course of action we should seek for the example set by Jesus and pattern our actions after His. How did He pray and how much did He pray and what did He pray for? He prayed from the cradle to the grave. After His baptism and before He entered His public ministry He went into the wilderness and fasted and prayed for forty days. He knew the life of service and suffering that lay ahead of Him and He sought strength for that life. Often He spent the whole night in prayer and often, when the disciples were still asleep, He prayed in the early hours of the dawn. He prayed at the grave of Lazarus. Before any great undertaking we also ought to go to God in prayer.

His most earnest prayers were offered in the garden of Gethsemane. So great was His agony there that we are told that His sweat was like blood falling to the ground.

> For me it was in the garden
> He prayed, "Not My will, but Thine";
> He had no tears for His own griefs,
> But sweat drops of blood for mine.

Then we hear Him as He prays on the cross. There He hangs, suffering physically, mentally and spiritually as no man has ever suffered. But did He pray for Himself? Did He pray that He might be relieved of suffering? Did He pray for vengeance upon those who were killing Him? No, He asked nothing for Himself. He prayed for His persecutors, "Father, forgive them, for they know not what they do." Yes, His life was a life of prayer. If Jesus who was perfect needed prayer, how much more do we sinners need to pray? If Jesus who had all power in heaven and earth needed to pray, how much more do we weaklings need to pray?

II. Prayer Is the First Thing Necessary for a Revival

There never has been a great revival, except that it was preceded by a season of earnest prayer. After Jesus went back to heaven the disciples, as He had commanded, began to pray for the power of the Holy Spirit to fall upon them. They prayed for a day, for two days, for five days, and nothing happened. After they had prayed for ten days the power came, their prayers were answered and three thousand souls were

saved in a day. But the revival at Pentecost was preceded by prayer.

In 1857 a great revival stirred America. Thousands
of souls were swept into the kingdom of God. At the
height of the revival someone decided to find out where
it began. They learned that one man in New York, who
had an hour for lunch each day, spent half of that time
pleading with God for a nation-wide revival. Soon he
was joined by others and then others and in a few
months large groups were meeting every day at noon
and praying for revival. And God answered and the fire
fell and souls were saved and churches revived.

Dr. L. R. Scarborough of Texas told of going to a
certain place to conduct a revival. He arrived just before eleven o'clock on Sunday morning and rushed over
to the church for the first service. As he started up the
steps a little woman plucked at his coat sleeve and said
to him, "Are you the preacher who is going to conduct
our revival?" He told her that he was. Then she said,
"I know we are going to have a great revival. For
months I have been getting up before dawn and praying for God to send us a great revival. And this morning, while my family was asleep and I was on my knees,
God seemed to whisper to me and tell me that He
was going to give us a mighty revival." And Dr. Scarborough said that during the revival he saw scores of
people come to Christ, and that when the heavenly
rewards were given out for service rendered during the
revival, this woman would receive the major share.

Do I hear someone saying, "We don't have revivals
now like we did in other days"? Well, the Bible tells us
that "we have not because we ask not." Maybe our
revivals of today are not like the revivals of other days
because we don't pray for revivals as we did then. I
have heard men tell of how they often prayed all night

in those days for a visitation of the Lord. They would get some lost person on their hearts and pray through the nights and days for them. No wonder God sent revival.

My first pastorate was in a small church in Atlanta. I had been there only a short time when they asked me to conduct a revival in the little church. It was a two-week meeting. In the first week of the meeting a number of people were saved who were all related and who lived in several houses near the church. One night they asked me to come to one of the homes after church for a prayer meeting. I went to that home and we sat in a circle in the living room. We prayed around the circle and I noticed that the burden of their prayers was for one of their number, a young man who had gone deep into sin. They didn't even know where he was, but they prayed that the Lord would bring him home and save him before the meetings ended. To their great delight and astonishment he came home on the Saturday before the meetings closed on Sunday. He surprised them by promising to go to church with them on Sunday night. That night the little church was packed with people and he had to sit in an open window at the rear of the church. After the message, when the invitation was given, this young man came weeping down the aisle to give his heart to the Saviour. He was gloriously converted. He had been away in another state but some unseen force, which he could not understand, impelled him to come back home. I believe that God, in answer to those earnest prayers, brought him home and brought him to Jesus.

Some years ago I was in a revival in a South Carolina town. On the last night of the meetings I looked over the congregation and noticed that a number of the most faithful members were not present. The chairman of the deacons, the Sunday school superintendent, and others were missing. But that night I felt an unusual spiritual power in the service. God helped me to preach, and when I gave the invitation eighteen people responded to the invitation to come to Christ, one of them a prominent lawyer I had witnessed to that day. After the benediction was pronounced one of the side doors in the auditorium opened up and a group of people came out, including these faithful members I had missed from the service. All the time that I had been preaching and giving the invitation, these people in that room had been praying for the power of God to fall upon the service. No wonder so many found Christ that night.

III. What Are We to Pray For in a Revival?

1. *We are to pray for ourselves.* God says, "If my people, which are called by my name, shall humble themselves, and pray, and seek my face . . . then will I hear from heaven, and will forgive their sin, and will heal their land" (II Chronicles 7:14). We need first of all, as Christians, to get right with God in every way. We need to draw a circle about ourselves and ask God to send a revival in that circle. Unless we are living clean, consecrated, dedicated Christian lives ourselves, we can never expect to influence anyone else.

> When Jesus came to Golgotha, they hanged Him on
>   a tree,
> They drove great nails through hands and feet, and
>   made a Calvary;
> They crowned Him with a crown of thorns, red were
>   His wounds and deep,
> For those were crude and cruel days, and human
>   flesh was cheap.

When Jesus came to Birmingham, they simply passed
  Him by,
They never hurt a hair of Him, they only let Him die;
For men had grown more tender, and they would not
  give Him pain,
They only just passed down the street, and left Him
  in the rain.

Still Jesus cried, "Forgive them, for they know not
  what they do,"
And still it rained the winter rain that drenched Him
  through and through;
The crowds went home and left the streets without
  a soul to see,
And Jesus crouched against a wall and cried for
  Calvary.

                    — *G. A. Studdert-Kennedy*

And today, as we see His own people turning away
from Him and going in so many other directions, I
wonder if He would not rather go to Calvary again
than to suffer their treatment of Him.

David said, "If I regard iniquity in my heart, the
Lord will not hear me." Before revival comes we must
humble ourselves before God, confess all of our sin and
clean up our lives. We may not be great sinners, but
in our hearts there is malice .and envy and jealousy
and many other sins. We can so easily see sin in others
but not in ourselves. We need to pray that God will
show us our own sins, that we might cry out to Him
for forgiveness.

In the early days of my ministry I served a church
in a small town in North Carolina. There was a private
hospital in the town and on several occasions I was
permitted to go into the operating room and observe
an operation. One day I went into that room with the
surgeon and he had me put on a robe and a mask and
stand over to one side. Then he "scrubbed up," put

on his robe and mask and rubber gloves and started toward the operating table. As he passed me I touched his arm with one finger and asked him a question. He answered me quite abruptly, then he said, "Now I'll have to 'scrub up' again." He went back to the basin, washed his hands in germicidal soap, put on a fresh robe and mask and another pair of gloves and proceeded with the operation. Now, why did he go to all of that trouble? He was afraid that in my touching him a germ might have passed from my finger to his robe, and that the germ might have been transmitted to the body of his patient, maybe causing further complications or death.

Well, we are dealing with something infinitely more valuable than a human body, for we are dealing with immortal souls. We must be clean in every way, lest something sinful in our lives should hurt one of these who need our Saviour. So I say that, if we expect revival to come, we must pray for ourselves, that God would help us to be what we ought to be.

2. *We are to pray for the power of the Holy Spirit.* It is "Not by might, nor by power, but by my spirit, saith the Lord of hosts" (Zechariah 4:6). We must have that power or we will have only a meeting and not a real revival. We must pray for that power to fall upon the preacher, the singer, the congregation, and in conviction upon lost sinners.

One time I was conducting a revival in my own church. Two girls, sixteen and eighteen years of age, had been attending our services. Neither was a Christian. Their salvation lay heavy on my heart and I decided to go over one afternoon and talk to them about the matter. I took my music director with me, but before we left my study we got on our knees and asked God to send the Holy Spirit before us to prepare the way and to fill our hearts so we could know what to say. When we rang the doorbell of their home both girls came to the door and invited us in. When we told them why we were there they said they had been thinking seriously about their salvation. In a few minutes, after explanation and Scripture reading and prayer, they had given their hearts to Jesus the Saviour.

The Holy Spirit had gone with us and before us and had done His work in their hearts. Luke 11:13 says, "If ye then, being evil, know how to give good gifts unto your children: how much more shall your heavenly Father give the Holy Spirit to them that ask him?"

3. *We are to pray for lost souls.* In your business life, in your circle of friends or maybe even in your own home there are those who don't know the Saviour. Do you pray for them? Do you storm the gates of heaven in their behalf? God has heard many prayers for the unsaved. An old song says, "Mother's prayers have followed me." And I am sure many prodigal sons have been brought to the Father's house because of the prayers of a mother or some other interested Christian.

In one of our cities a boy fell into sin and was finally arrested for a crime he had committed. The pastor of the boy's mother went out to see her and to try to bring her a bit of consolation. However, she would not be comforted. She kept on saying, "It's all my fault, it's all my fault." When the pastor questioned her she said, "Before we moved to the city I prayed for my boy morning, noon and night. But since coming here I have been involved in a busy social life and I have neglected my spiritual life and have failed to pray for my boy. As long as I prayed for him there was no trouble, but this tragedy has come because I haven't prayed for him." And who knows but that she was right.

When I found the Lord at sixteen I began to pray

for the salvation of one of my older brothers. He wandered over many parts of the country and, seemingly, had no thought for the things of God. But I kept on praying for him. Later I entered the ministry and I not only prayed for him, but I sought to win him to Christ. Then, after I had prayed for him for eighteen years, one night when I preached and gave the invitation, he came forward to confess Christ as his personal Saviour. Eighteen years of prayer, then God answered! And when I conducted his funeral several years ago I was glad I had not ceased to pray for him over the years.

Now our prayers for the lost are to be prayers of compassionate agony. "They that sow in tears shall reap in joy. He that goeth forth and weepeth, bearing precious seed, shall doubtless come again with rejoicing, bringing his sheaves with him" (Psalm 126:5, 6). "For as soon as Zion travailed, she brought forth her children" (Isaiah 66:8). Yes, it is when we pray with compassion, it is when the tears fall, that souls are saved.

Years ago, when I was quite a young preacher, I held a meeting in a small Southern town. Another young preacher led the singing. We became acquainted with a young man in the town who was not a Christian. He attended the services and we witnessed to him, but he made no response. One night, when the singer and I were praying together before going to bed, each of us felt led to pray for that young man. But when we came to bring his name before God, each of us broke down and sobbed, so great was our concern for him and our desire to see him saved. The next night when I gave the invitation he was the first one to come forward to confess Christ as his Saviour. The years sped by, and one day I received a newspaper clipping through the mail telling me that the young man had been killed in a tragic automobile accident. Then I could not help but stop and thank God that we had wept over him in prayer, sowing God's seed in tears.

In later years I conducted a meeting in the Central Baptist Church of Waycross, Georgia. I preached at the church each night and each morning in Piedmont Institute, a small Baptist school near the city. During the meeting many of the students gave their hearts to the Saviour. On Thursday morning I said to the students, "Tomorrow morning I will come to hold my last service with you. I hope you'll be praying for that service." After that Thursday morning service was over some of the students said to me, "There are still two unsaved boys left in the school. We are going to pray for them to be saved tomorrow and we want you to pray also." So that night the pastor and I prayed for those boys, then we tumbled into bed and went to sleep.

On Friday morning when we stepped on the campus some of the students met us and they were rejoicing that the two boys had already surrendered to Christ and were ready to make their public profession of faith that morning. These students told me that the night before they had gathered in the boys' dormitory to pray for these two unsaved lads. As they were praying, at twenty minutes past midnight, they heard a knock on the door. Someone opened the door and one of the unsaved boys was standing there. He said, "I want to be a Christian, tell me if I can be saved tonight." They soon led him to Christ and he joined them in prayer for the other boy. In the wee hours of the morning, there came another knock on the door. The other unsaved boy came in and told how he could not sleep and how he, too, wanted to be saved. So in a few minutes the last student was saved and the little school was one hundred per cent for Christ. And it came about because of the compassionate, earnest, fervent prayers of some of God's young people.

In Matthew 18:19 we find the Lord's wonderful promise about covenant prayer, "Again I say unto you, that if two of you shall agree on earth as touching anything that they shall ask, it shall be done for thee of my Father which is in heaven."

The wonderful thing about this great promise is that it works. Let two people who love God and are living for Him get together and pray according to the will of God, and He promises them that their prayer will be answered. Why not try this plan? Why not claim this promise the Lord makes to His people?

Many years ago I held a meeting in a country church. Large congregations filled the building both morning and night and God was saving many precious souls. Then one day a man said to me, "Have you met Frank Christian?" I told him that I had not. "Well," said this man, "he is the worst sinner in our community. He has been to hear you preach a couple of times. He always comes to our meetings about twice, then he goes out in the community and says everything evil he can think of about our visiting preacher and our church." Then another man said, "But it hasn't been that way this time. Something seems to be happening to him. He seems different." Mr. Christian kept on coming to church. He bore the name but, from all that the people said, he was anything but a Christian.

The last night of the meeting came. I preached and gave the invitation and several people came forward for salvation. I saw this man in the aisle seat near the back of the church. I felt led to speak to him, so I went back and asked him if he didn't want to give his heart to Christ. He shook his head. Then I put my hands on his shoulder and I said, "My friend, if I were in your place I would cry out for God to 'be merciful to me, a sinner'." I went back to the pulpit and the song leader whispered to me, "If God can save that man He can save anybody in the world."

The invitation closed and we sang another song while the people came forward to shake hands with those who had been saved and joined the church during the meeting. As we sang the second verse Frank Christian came down the aisle, tears running down his cheeks. He said to the pastor, "Can you stop the song and let me get in that line? I want to be saved." The singing was stopped and Frank made his tearful profession of faith. In a moment his buddy, who had been sitting with him, came forward to give his heart to the Lord.

Then the singer said to me, "I believe it now, I believe God can save the worst sinner in the world." How true it is! God is willing to send a revival to any church that will pay the price in prayer and dedication. So I close as I began by saying that prayer is the biggest, the most important, the most needed thing in a revival.

Pine Creek Church Library